Contents

The Department of Energy

An Agency That Cannot Be Reinvented

Irwin Stelzer,
with Robert Patton

The AEI Press

Publisher for the American Enterprise Institute

WASHINGTON, D.C.

1996

Available in the United States from the AEI Press, c/o Publisher Resources Inc., 1224 Heil Quaker Blvd., P.O. Box 7001, La Vergne, Tenn. 37086-7001. Distributed outside the United States by arrangement with Eurospan, 3 Henrietta Street, London, WC2E 8LU England.

ISBN 0-8447-7054-x

1 3 5 7 9 10 8 6 4 2

THE AEI PRESS
Publisher for the American Enterprise Institute
1150 17th Street, N.W., Washington, D.C. 20036

Printed in the United States of America

SUMMARY

The Department of Energy cannot be "reinvented." It should be abolished, its defense-related functions transferred to an independent, civilian-controlled agency, its interventions in energy markets terminated, its oil- and power-producing and marketing assets privatized, and its research functions rationalized by an independent commission.

Our reasons for these conclusions include the following:

• The department has demonstrated its inability to discharge its defense-related cleanup function in an efficient manner, resulting in enormous waste in the view of Vice President Al Gore's National Performance Review, the Army Corps of Engineers, a recent report commissioned by the Senate, and most disinterested observers. Furthermore, Secretary Hazel O'Leary's claim to have made "impressive progress" in turning the program around is not supported by persuasive evidence.

• Changes in energy markets have resulted in the minimization of the market failures that initially were used to justify the department's subsidization of various energy-producing technologies and of energy conservation.

• The department is incapable of distinguishing research areas in which government funding is appropriate from those in which it is not; as a consequence, it has expanded its research activities beyond those made necessary by market failure, and the possibility exists of rationalizing federal expenditures through a series of privatizations and facilities closures.

- There is widespread agreement that the assets the department manages should be privatized to eliminate uneconomic and discriminatory subsidies to some energy consumers and to place oil reserves in the private sector.

These conclusions arise from an analysis of the department's activities rather than from any antigovernment ideology or mere desire to reduce government spending: they would be no different were the federal budget now in surplus. They were first vetted in an earlier, widely circulated draft to elicit comments from DOE, among others. Those comments, to the extent pertinent, are reflected in this final version.

1

Introduction

There are two ways in which to develop a position on the future of the Department of Energy. One is to rely on ideology—either the ideology that finds a role for government in all economic affairs or the contrary belief that any reduction in the size of government is good and the elimination of an entire cabinet department even better.

The better method of deciding the future of DOE, in our view, is to look to the reasons it was initially established to determine whether those reasons remain compelling today; to examine the missions of the department, both those imposed on it by legislation and those developed by the department itself in the inevitable process of self-aggrandizement characteristic of non–market-driven bureaucracies (and, until markets force adjustments, some private sector organizations); and, finally, to decide whether those functions that must be performed by government, and are now housed in DOE, can most efficiently be executed by that cabinet-level department.

We begin this exploration with two assumptions. First, we do not deny the integrity or devotion of any of the secretaries who have led DOE. All have had difficult tasks assigned to them by a succession of presidents and Congresses; all have tried to improve the efficiency of the department. The latest such effort has taken DOE through "an intense period of fundamental rethinking," during which it gathered up "compelling ideas" from its "Strategic Alignment Team" and produced "a bold action plan" reflecting "tough decisions." This is DOE's answer to those who favor "dismantling the department and possibly even terminating further public support for our missions."[1]

Second, we have no ideological commitment either to the retention or to the abolition of DOE. If the department retains a valid mission and is the best instrument for the efficient accomplishment of that mission, it would sacrifice reason and efficiency to ideology and political posturing to abolish it. If, however, it has become a bureaucracy in search of a mission, or one that has demonstrated an inability to cope with the legitimate problems before it, it should go, with its necessary functions transferred to another institution or institutions.

---

1. U.S. Department of Energy, "Message from the Secretary," *Saving Dollars and Making Sense: Strategic Alignment and Downsizing,* May 1995, pp. i, ii.

2

History of DOE

K nowledge of the history of DOE—the reasons it was
establihed and how it has coped with the problems
before it—is helpful in deciding its future role. Do
the reasons for the department's establishment remain
compelling? Has it demonstrated an ability to discharge
its obligations efficiently?

The Antecedents of DOE

The Department of Energy was created in 1977, by President Jimmy Carter, with the approval of both houses of Congress.[1] But it did not spring full-blown from President Carter's head. Rather, it was the culmination of long-standing government involvement in the energy industries, an involvement that included such diverse activities as providing electrical energy directly to entire regions through such instruments as the Tennessee Valley Authority, fathering the technology that was essential to the development of commercial nuclear power, favoring domestic oil producers with special tax advantages (the famous depletion allowance), imposing price controls on natural gas, and otherwise dab-

---

1. Unless otherwise noted, facts relating to the history of DOE and its predecessor agencies are taken from Terrence R. Fehner and Jack M. Holl's valuable *Department of Energy 1977–1994: A Summary History* (Oak Ridge, Tenn.: U.S. Department of Energy, Office of Scientific and Technical Information, November 1994).

bling in an industry in which politics and economics have generally been inseparable. By incorporating the nation's defense-related nuclear activities into the new department, Carter also continued the strategy—begun with the "atoms for peace" initiative of the Eisenhower administration—of pooling scientific research for nuclear weapons with that for civilian nuclear reactors, as well as the policy of keeping the production of nuclear weapons outside of the military.

These federal interventions in energy markets did not lead to the demand for a cabinet-level department until 1971, when President Nixon, concerned about what he saw as the fragility of the nation's energy supply, established the Special Energy Committee, a group of presidential advisers, and the National Energy Office, charged with coordinating energy policy between agencies.

In June of 1973, Nixon created the Energy Policy Office, which merged the functions of the Special Energy Committee and the National Energy Office and added new ones. At that time, he also called for the creation of an agency to coordinate energy research and sought to tap new sources of energy by building a pipeline to Alaska's oil reserves. Finally, Nixon called for deregulation of natural gas prices to provide producers with a greater incentive to find and produce natural gas.

Then came the first oil embargo. In October 1973, in response to America's support for Israel in the Yom Kippur War, the Organization of Petroleum Exporting Countries (OPEC) unsheathed its oil weapon and announced an embargo on oil shipments to the United States. Nixon reacted swiftly. First, in an address to the nation on November 7, he announced Project Independence: "Let us set as our national goal . . . that by the end of this decade we will have developed the potential to meet our own energy needs without depending on any foreign sources."[2]

---

2. Richard Nixon, "Address to the Nation about Policies to Deal with the Energy Shortages," November 7, 1973. At that time, imported oil accounted for a bit less than 35 percent of U.S. oil supplies; it now accounts for more than half.

Then, in December, Nixon replaced the Energy Policy Office with the Federal Energy Office. The new agency's expanded powers included allocation and price controls for oil and gasoline. On May 4, 1974, Nixon signed a bill creating the Federal Energy Administration, described in DOE's official history as "a temporary agency to meet with the immediate, and presumably temporary, energy crisis."[3] This agency took over the functions of the Federal Energy Office and would exist until its role was subsumed into the Department of Energy in 1977.

Despite the lifting of the oil embargo, President Ford continued his predecessor's quest for energy independence. Ford focused on encouraging the development of domestic energy sources by calling for an easing of restrictions on domestic coal use, greater incentives for oil exploration, and the development of nuclear power and synthetic fuels. In October 1974, he signed the Energy Reorganization Act of 1974, which created the Energy Research and Development Administration to take over the research functions of the Atomic Energy Commission, disbanded by the act, and of other federal agencies.

The act also created both the Nuclear Regulatory Commission, which took over the regulatory functions of the Atomic Energy Commission, and a national energy board called the Energy Resources Council. The council's function, as Ford put it, was "developing a single national energy policy and program,"[4] a statement of purpose quite similar to what would later be the stated mission of DOE. The council included the heads of the Federal Energy Administration and the Energy Research and Development Administration, the two organizations that Jimmy Carter would later merge to form DOE. In 1975, Ford signed the Energy Policy and Conservation Act. This act extended price controls on oil for four years, introduced auto fuel efficiency standards, and provided for the creation of what is now the Strategic Petroleum Reserve.

---

3. Fehner and Holl, *Department of Energy 1977–1994*, p. 17.
4. Ibid., p. 18.

It is useful to pause before considering the culmination of this increasing involvement of government in the energy industries. Why were Republican presidents, supposedly devotees of free markets and limited government, drawn into creating a new government bureaucracy?

In part, of course, President Nixon had quite an expansive view of the role of government (witness his eventual use of price controls to fight inflation), resulting in policies his successor had neither the mandate nor the time to change. In part, too, the alphabet soup of agencies came into being because reliable energy supplies are crucial to both the nation's economic well-being and its national security, because supply interruptions are costly, and because market responses to such interruptions are regarded as too slow and uncertain in producing solutions to be relied on by politicians under pressure to "do something." So, when an event arguably labeled an "energy crisis" occurs, government intervenes.

It is not unfair to say that this lack of faith in market mechanisms has been bipartisan. The notion that prices should be free to match energy supply with demand, or to determine who should use what fuels, where, in what quantities, and at what cost, was not widely held in the 1970s. Indeed, increases in energy prices were deemed to be certain to cause the premature termination of political careers.

So, rather than rely on markets, President Carter's predecessors relied on government, thereby laying the organizational groundwork for the creation of DOE, the cabinet-level energy or natural resources department for which both Nixon and Ford had called. The creation of the Federal Energy Administration under Nixon centralized federal energy policy, and the creation of the Energy Research and Development Administration under Ford brought previously scattered federal energy research and development into a single agency. Ford's creation of the Energy Resources Council, a national board that included the heads of both these agencies, was the penultimate step to a cabinet-level energy department.

Carter Creates DOE—"Moral Equivalent of War"

Jimmy Carter made energy policy a top priority. Shortly after taking office, he signed the Emergency Natural Gas Act of 1977, declaring the current shortage of natural gas a national emergency. He appointed former Atomic Energy Commission chairman James Schlesinger "energy czar," and, in October, after Congress passed Carter's Department of Energy Organization Act, Schlesinger became the first secretary of energy.

Along with the Federal Energy Administration and the Energy Research and Development Administration, DOE inherited energy-related functions of the Departments of Defense, Interior, Agriculture, Commerce, Housing and Urban Development, and Transportation. The Federal Energy Regulatory Commission (FERC) was also established as an independent agency within DOE, combining the functions of the now-defunct Federal Power Commission with certain regulatory functions of the Interstate Commerce Commission. In short, the grab-bag of energy programs that had been accumulating for over a decade became DOE's responsibility, along with management of the nuclear stockpile and development of new weapons.

Contemporary reaction was mixed. The *New York Times*, in a March 1977 lead editorial entitled "A Fair Fast Start on Energy," lauded Carter for addressing the "urgent matter" of the "adoption of a long-term energy policy." Expressing optimism about the new agency's "difficult but vital bureaucratic arrangements," the *Times* concluded, "President Carter is right to invest the prestige he brought to the White House in the creation of an Energy Department and the objectives it will pursue."[5] But *Newsweek*, noting the growth of federal energy programs since 1973, fretted about the "bureaucratic penchant for expansion" and opined that the new agency "seems even less controllable

---

5. "A Fair Fast Start on Energy," *New York Times*, March 3, 1977.

than most."[6] And Milton Friedman, even more nervous, called the new agency "a Trojan Horse. . . . It enthrones a bureaucracy that would have a self-interest in expanding in size and power and would have the means to do so—both directly, through exercising price control and other powers, and indirectly, through propagandizing the public and the Congress for still broader powers."[7]

Carter called the challenge of energy policy "the moral equivalent of war" and produced a spate of new rules, regulations, and proposed legislation with which to wage that war. Unlike Nixon and Ford, whose reaction to perceived shortages and supply cutoffs was, in the main, to encourage the development of new domestic energy sources—to increase supply—Carter emphasized conservation—a reduction in demand. In part, this emphasis stemmed from his general view that Americans consumed too much. "Too many of us," he said in an address to the nation, "now tend to worship self-indulgence and consumption . . . piling up material goods cannot fill the emptiness of lives which have no confidence or purpose."[8] This was entirely consistent with his view that energy policy, as the moral equivalent of war, was to be won by establishing a new conservation "ethic." From this philosophy, not peculiar to President Carter, it is an easy step to federal regulations governing how fast we may drive, how cool and warm we may keep ourselves, and how and of what materials we shall build our homes.

Carter, however, did not completely ignore the supply side of the energy equation: he proposed programs to subsidize the development of nonconventional energy sources and eased price controls on domestic crude oil.

It is worth pausing here to consider the underlying basis for the increased role of DOE in energy markets shortly after its founding, not primarily to comment on

---

6. "Birth of a Superagency," *Newsweek,* July 11, 1977, p. 59.

7. Milton Friedman, "A Department of Energy?" *Newsweek,* May 23, 1977, p. 62.

8. Jimmy Carter, "Address to the Nation," July 15, 1979, p. 4 (mimeo).

the efficacy of such intervention at the time but instead to shed some light on the propriety of the department's continuing role in these markets.

In the late 1970s and early 1980s, energy markets suffered from three serious imperfections:

• First, prices did not reflect the externalities involved in energy use. The driver filling his tank did not, when he paid for gasoline, cover the cost of crude oil supply interruptions; the coal-burning factory did not bear the cost of the pollutants it emitted into the atmosphere.

• Second, energy prices did not reflect the true economic, or marginal, costs of production.[9] Government regulation prevented natural gas prices from reaching market-clearing levels in the interstate market; a hodgepodge of federal and state regulations distorted oil markets; electric utilities and their regulators adhered to a pricing system based on noneconomic concepts such as fully allocated costs. As a result, consumers were receiving price signals that were inaccurate reflectors of the costs of their energy consumption.

• Third, good information concerning the relative costs of consuming energy and of conserving it were not widely available, energy being so cheap before the oil price "spikes" that there was little need for such information. This made it difficult for consumers to make intelligent choices, to cite one example, between turning up their thermostats and adding insulation to their attics—a problem compounded by the failure of most utilities to price electricity and gas at their marginal cost.

Such market failure arguably provided a basis for government intervention—especially in an era in which regulatory failure was not a well-recognized danger. But the market imperfections of the late 1970s and early 1980s have been eliminated: oil and gas prices are no longer reg-

9. In this connection, see Alfred E. Kahn, *The Economics of Regulation: Principles and Institutions* (New York: John Wiley & Sons, Inc., 1970), pp. 63ff.

ulated; marginal cost pricing has become widespread in the utility industries; externalities have largely been internalized, with the notable exception of those associated with reliance on imported oil;[10] consumers are now well informed as to the trade-offs between the use and the conservation of energy. In short, however sound the reasons for expanding the role of government in energy markets may have been when Presidents Nixon, Ford, and Carter were in office—and that case for intervention was, even then, seriously flawed—those reasons no longer exist to support a continuation of DOE activities in these areas.

DOE since Carter—Shifting Priorities

Reagan. President Reagan's first inclination was to dismantle DOE. He failed—no surprise to students of the capacity of bureaucracies to create constituencies that ensure their longevity. Congress opposed turning the nuclear weapons program over to the military, and efforts to parcel out DOE functions to other agencies ran into the inevitable roadblocks in Congress, with no committee willing to cede jurisdiction over DOE activities to another. Furthermore, energy issues were no longer at the top of the national agenda. According to DOE's official history, published in 1994, efforts to dismantle the department "languished . . . through summer and fall 1982. The national economy, the federal budget, and the November elections dominated the congressional agenda."[11] This was the case despite the finding of the Congressional Budget Office and General Accounting Office that DOE dismantlement would result in savings, dismissed by Secretary O'Leary as "at most a few million dollars per year."[12]

---

10. See William W. Hogan, "The $200 Billion Surprise: Energy Security and the Oil Tariff," Discussion paper, Energy and Environmental Policy Center, Harvard University, July 1987 (mimeo).
11. Fehner and Holl, *Department of Energy 1977–1994*, p. 36.
12. Hazel O'Leary, "The Department of Energy: Why Abolishment Makes No Sense," *Energy Daily*, July, 21, 1995, p. 6.

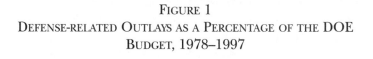

FIGURE 1
DEFENSE-RELATED OUTLAYS AS A PERCENTAGE OF THE DOE
BUDGET, 1978–1997

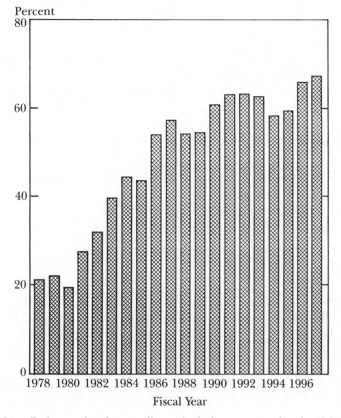

NOTE: Defense-related expenditures include weapons-related activities and the weapons complex cleanup. The figure for 1997 is DOE's request to Congress.
SOURCE: U.S. Department of Energy, Office of Budget.

Reagan therefore reordered DOE priorities. Although his budget for DOE remained at about the same level as Carter's, the department's resources were redirected toward the nuclear weapons program and the Strategic Defense Initiative, thus providing the administration with a de facto increase in the military budget (see figure 1).

And attention was shifted away from Carter's programs to limit the demand for energy back to the Nixon-Ford efforts to increase supply. Needless to say, remaining price controls on oil and gasoline were removed as part of a general program to reassert the role of market forces in the energy industries and to eliminate distortions stemming from price and allocation regulations.[13]

Note, however, that Reagan's stated belief in relying on market forces did not translate into a completely hands-off policy. Energy markets are tempting targets for proponents of various technologies, the development of which the private sector is unwilling to finance. Just as Carter chose to subsidize "renewable" sources of energy, Reagan's DOE chose to subsidize the development of technologies that would reduce the environmental impact of using the fossil fuels that Carter so disfavored. These subsidies aside, the Reagan DOE devoted fewer resources to market interventions and more to the defense activities that came to claim an increasing share of the department's budget.

Bush. Under President Bush, DOE continued the now-traditional Republican policies of attempting to expand domestic energy supply, primarily by opening new areas to oil exploitation. During those years, DOE also began the cleanup of nuclear weapons sites: along with other defense-related expenditures, that activity consumed well over half of DOE's budget. The name of the game was catch-up: environmental considerations had been poorly understood, or ignored. Admiral James Watkins, Bush's energy secretary, pointed out that health and safety considerations had been sacrificed to maximize production goals and that the entire program had been wrapped in a blanket of "collegial secrecy."[14]

---

13. U.S. Department of Energy, *Energy Security: A Report to the President of the United States,* March 1987, p. 214.
14. Fehner and Holl, *Department of Energy 1977–1994,* p. 54.

Paradoxically, DOE's past failures were given as the reason for its continued existence: with so much work to be done, it was unthinkable, said Watkins, to consider DOE "redundant," or to suppose that "its responsibilities could be taken over by others."[15]

But the department's natural instinct for survival cannot, alone, explain its durability during twelve years of market-oriented Republican administrations. Nor does its role as supplement to the military budget account for its durability. Other forces were at work.

First, some government agency had to exist to discharge the obligations created by legislation. The president, for example, is required by law to submit a biennial national energy policy plan to Congress. And the Energy Policy Act, signed by Bush in 1992, required, as then-Deputy Secretary Linda Stuntz pointed out, sixty-one reports, twenty-one solicitations, fifteen regulations, eight programs, and four advisory panels.[16]

Another explanation of the department's durability is the link between energy and national security and America's reliance on foreign oil—much of it produced in one of the world's least stable regions, the Middle East, a region to which America has very recently had to send a half-million troops and which even now threatens to explode as a result of renewed terrorist activities. Policy makers are rightly nervous about the willingness of OPEC's Arab members to use their "oil weapon" to disrupt the world's economy, in response to unpredictable political events. But politicians shy away from market-oriented solutions to this vulnerability. So the Democrats among them hunt for regulations that will curtail America's energy consumption and subsidies that will encourage the development of renewables such as solar and wind power, sources they anyhow prefer for environmental reasons. Meanwhile, some Republicans prefer to subsidize

---

15. Ibid., p. 55.
16. Ibid., p. 72.

nuclear power and the use of coal as alternatives to foreign oil. Naturally, regulations must be administered and subsidies paid out. That requires a department to do the regulating and paying. Hence, the ability of DOE to survive even the onslaught of the market-oriented Reagan administration and to accommodate itself to the agendas of successive administrations.

Clinton. Under President Clinton and Energy Secretary Hazel O'Leary, the emphasis of energy policy shifted back to conservation and to environmental concerns such as global warming. Expenditures on the nuclear weapons cleanup continued to grow, as did outlays to stimulate technology transfers between DOE and industry, academia, and others, in pursuit of what has come to be known as "industrial competitiveness," now offered as the justification for a variety of programs, just as "national security" was in the days of the cold war.[17]

As is to be expected, the Department of Energy has found an important role for itself—what Secretary O'Leary describes as a "new national agenda"—in the post–energy crisis, post–cold war era. DOE's new goals, said O'Leary in 1994, include "fueling a competitive economy, improving the environment through waste management and pollution prevention, reducing the nuclear danger, and sustainable energy development."[18] The first of these includes that hardy perennial: "helping guard against supply disruptions"; the second involves cleaning up radioactive and hazardous waste sites; the third, dismantling some nuclear weapons and ensuring the safety of others; and the last includes R & D.[19]

---

17. See, for example, U.S. Department of Energy, *Fueling a Competitive Economy: Strategic Plan,* April 1994, pp. 12–14.

18. U.S. Department of Energy, *1994 Accomplishments,* p. 1. Some of these new goals are, in reality, traditional Democratic energy policy goals dressed in new language.

19. U.S. Department of Energy, *Saving Dollars and Making Sense,* pp. 1–2.

3

DOE Today—
A Giant under Siege

A recent DOE publication asks, *U.S. Department of Energy: What Is It? What Does It Do?* It attempts to answer the questions it put to itself with the following statement of the department's mission:

> The Department of Energy is entrusted to contribute to the welfare of the Nation by providing the scientific foundation, technology, policy and institutional leadership necessary to achieve efficiency in energy use, diversity in energy sources, a more productive and competitive economy, improved environmental quality, and a secure national defense.[1]

Clearly, so expansive a view of its mission well places the department to do just about what it pleases.

It is beyond the scope of this analysis to examine, *in detail,* whether DOE discharges each of its responsibilities efficiently. A suggestion that it has not done so comes from Secretary O'Leary: last year she announced plans to save DOE more than $14.1 billion over five years, includ-

---

1. U.S. Department of Energy, *U.S. Department of Energy: What Is It? What Does It Do?* (n.d.).

ing $4.4 billion from the weapons-complex cleanup; $1.2 billion from applied research; almost $2.9 billion by a "strategic realignment" of DOE's various departments, including the layoff of nearly a quarter of DOE's federal employees; and almost $5.6 billion from the sale of DOE assets. It is, of course, true, as Secretary O'Leary has argued, that these "cost-cutting reforms [are] . . . precisely what the American public wants from its government ."[2] But it is also true that (1) the *need* for such cuts demonstrates the existence of considerable fat in an organization she has now headed for over three years; (2) the savings promised—just over a billion and a half dollars per year from a baseline budget of $18 billion—are hardly the massive "downsizing" the DOE press release trumpets; (3) nowhere has DOE compared the value of the missions it has chosen to retain, or their scale, with the value of other government programs that are being sharply curtailed; (4) counting the sale of assets as savings, as DOE does, is a peculiar sort of accounting; and (5) most of the promised savings are to be realized in future years, if at all. In fact, DOE conceded earlier this year that two-thirds of the "savings" that were to come from asset sales will not be realized in the near future.[3]

Nevertheless, O'Leary's proposal shows that even the DOE hierarchy is not prepared to defend the department's current level of efficiency. Unfortunately, neither is it prepared to address the fundamental questions: Do we need a Department of Energy? Can some of its functions be hived off to agencies that might better perform them? Can other functions be eliminated entirely?

To answer these questions, we must consider each of DOE's current responsibilities, which fall into two broad categories: military and civilian.

---

2. O'Leary, "The Department of Energy: Why Abolishment Makes No Sense," p. 5.

3. Pamela Newman, "Curtis: No PMA Sale in '97 Budget," *Energy Daily,* January 23, 1996, p. 4.

Military Programs

Most of DOE's budget goes to management of environmental problems associated with nuclear weapons production and to national security functions.

Environmental Management. There can be no question that the dangerous radioactive debris from the nation's nuclear weapons program left at more than 120 sites around the country must be cleaned up.[4] This is the responsibility of DOE's Office of Environmental Management (EM) and will consume $5.5 billion of DOE's 1996 budget of $16.3 billion, making it the department's largest program.

EM is charged with cleaning up the waste produced by the nuclear weapons production of the past fifty years. It defines its goals as nuclear material and facility stabilization, environmental restoration, waste management, and the development of technologies related to the cleanup effort:

- *Nuclear material and facility stabilization* is the removal and stabilizing of highly radioactive material from weapons production-related facilities, including protecting weapons-ready material from theft by would-be terrorists.[5]

- *Environmental restoration* is the cleanup of the nuclear and nonnuclear military waste. DOE describes environmental restoration as including "a wide range of activities such as stabilizing contaminated soil; treating ground water; decontaminating and decommissioning nuclear reactors and process buildings, including chemical separation plants; and exhuming buried waste."[6] This program of environmental restoration consumes about a third of EM's budget.

---

4. Of the more than 120 sites at which DOE cleans up and treats waste, one, Hanford, accounts for nearly one-third of the cleanup budget; five account for about two-thirds, and ten for 80 percent.

5. U.S. Department of Energy, Office of Environmental Management, *Estimating the Cold War Mortgage: The 1995 Baseline Environmental Report,* March 1995, pp. 2.13–2.15.

6. Ibid., pp. 2.7–2.9.

TABLE 1
Number of Federal Employees, Contract Workers, and Contractors per Employee at DOE, EPA, and EM, March 1996

	Federal Employees	Contract Workers	Contractors per Employee
Department of Energy	15,500	76,600	4.9
Environmental Protection Agency	16,600	9,000–10,000	0.5
Environmental Management	3,200	39,700	12.0

NOTE: Figures for DOE exclude EM. Figures for federal employees are as of early 1996. Figures for contract workers are as of late 1995.
SOURCES: U.S. Department of Energy and U.S. Environmental Protection Agency.

- *Waste management,* allotted just over a quarter of EM's funds in the department's 1996 budget, involves the treatment, storage, and disposal of radioactive, hazardous, and sanitary waste mostly generated by the weapons program.[7]
- *Technology development* for the cleanup effort is conducted at several of the national labs, at which technologies for treating and containing waste are developed.

EM relies heavily on contract workers, an arrangement that dates back to the Manhattan project. Under the government-owned, contractor-operated (GOCO) system, "the government owns all the land, facilities, and equipment, while the contractor manages the facility and employs research, development, and production personnel," as well as support and maintenance staff.[8] These con-

---

7. Ibid., pp. 2.9–2.13.
8. Office of the Vice President, *From Red Tape to Results: Creating a Government That Works Better and Costs Less: Department of Energy,* Accompanying report of the National Performance Review, September 1993, p. 19.

tract workers play a much larger role at EM than in other agencies, witness the comparison of EM with DOE (excluding EM) and the Environmental Protection Agency in table 1.

The use of contract workers is not *necessarily* inefficient, even if contract workers appear more expensive, by standard accounting measures, than federal employees. Workers with the skills necessary to perform the cleanup work, for example, may not be available to the government, an imperfection in the labor market perhaps explained by the rigidities in government hiring and wage policies. Or the work may be of a temporary or fluctuating nature, making it efficient to use contract workers, to whom the government has no long-term employment obligation. And it may indeed be possible that the nature of EM's work makes it feasible for each employee to supervise a dozen contract workers (see table 1).

In the end, the proof of the pudding is in the eating: Is the job getting done? And at reasonable cost? The answers seem to be no and no. The authorities for those answers range from Vice President Al Gore and his National Performance Review, to the General Accounting Office, the Office of Management and Budget, the U.S. Army Corps of Engineers, the Office of Technology Assessment, and DOE itself. Furthermore, the persistence of the failure suggests that the problem is intrinsic to the culture of DOE and to its operating procedures and that the cultures and procedures are not capable of reform. As the General Accounting Office concluded last year, "Unfortunately, DOE's past history of contamination, along with its contracting problems, makes it unclear how successful DOE's new process will be."[9]

In 1987, in the wake of the accident at Chernobyl, Energy Secretary John S. Herrington commissioned the

---

9. Victor S. Rezendes, director, energy and science issues, U.S. General Accounting Office, Statement before the Subcommittee on Energy and Environment, Committee on Science, House of Representatives, February 13, 1995, p. 4 (mimeo).

National Research Council to study environmental and safety issues at DOE's weapons complex. The council reported major problems, which led indirectly to the establishment of the cleanup office (eventually called EM) in 1989. The council diagnosed the environmental and safety hazards in the weapons complex as stemming in part from "a loose-knit system of largely self-regulated contractors,"[10] exactly the problem that, almost a decade later, continues to plague the cleanup itself.

When Secretary Watkins took over DOE in 1989 and established what would become the Office of Environmental Management, he promised to update DOE's "antique" management style and create "a new culture of responsibility."[11] Two years later, however, the Office of Technology Assessment found that the "institutional resources and processes to make and implement sound, publicly acceptable decisions are not presently in place." In the absence of major changes, the report found that "effective cleanup of the weapons complex in the next several decades is unlikely."[12]

Nor does there seem to have been much improvement since that review. Early in Secretary O'Leary's tenure, Senator J. Bennett Johnston called the program "a grand and glorious mess . . . no function of government has been as mismanaged as our waste cleanup."[13]

This view was repeated, in somewhat less graphic terms, in the National Performance Review. It points out that "an interagency review by OMB and the U.S. Army Corps of Engineers . . . cited the lack of EM personnel with the appropriate skills as a primary reason for high contract costs."[14] And costs are more than marginally higher than

---

10. Fehner and Holl, *Department of Energy 1977–1994,* p. 47.
11. Ibid., pp. 53, 56.
12. U.S. Congress, Office of Technology Assessment, *Complex Cleanup: The Environmental Legacy of Nuclear Weapons Production,* OTA-O-484, February 1991, p. 9.
13. Fehner and Holl, *Department of Energy 1977–1994,* pp. 88.
14. Office of the Vice President, *From Red Tape to Results,* p. 7.

they should be. The report notes that DOE's review of its contractors' cleanup estimates produced substantially lower estimates than those of the contractors. And even DOE's estimate might be high. The vice president cites a 1992 Army Corps of Engineers audit that found:

> DOE's estimated costs were higher than the Corps estimates for comparable environmental restoration and waste management projects. Specifically, after a detailed evaluation of nearly $1 billion in spending (18 percent of the EM program), costs were found to be higher than the amounts the Corps would expect to pay for the same work by 42 percent. The primary difference in the estimates can be attributed to overhead and administrative costs that may be saved through changes in management and contracting procedures.[15]

The vice president's own assessment is even more damning:

> EM's fiscal year 1993 budget is $5.5 billion, much of which is spent on contracts (in fiscal year 1992, 67 percent of the total budget was expended on contracts). A former Assistant Secretary estimated that, due to wasteful and inefficient expenditures of funds, the program was operating at 60 to 65 percent efficiency. If this is the case, the program could waste $2 billion this year.[16]

Most knowledgeable observers say that DOE's use of management and operating (M&O) contractors is a major part of the problem. According to the National Performance

---

15. U.S. Department of the Army, Army Corps of Engineers, *Supplemental Report on Cost Estimates,* April 29, 1992, p. i, cited in Office of the Vice President, *From Red Tape to Results,* p. 8. We recognize, of course, that cost savings promised by a rival, mission-seeking agency are always suspect.
16. Office of the Vice President, *From Red Tape to Results,* p. 5.

Review, "M&Os are unique to DOE; they are issued a letter of credit that allows them to draw funds directly from the Treasury, and they are granted considerable latitude in deciding how to manage a DOE facility."[17] The vice president's review goes on to find that M&Os are "minimally accountable," that DOE has had a "traditionally lenient approach to M&O management," and that DOE contracts "provide little incentive to control costs."[18] Hardly a ringing endorsement from a source ideologically committed to the retention of DOE.

Secretary O'Leary responds that the National Performance Review was developed by the Clinton administration to identify and correct problems in DOE and other organizations. She writes that "since then, the program has undergone substantial change at all levels to improve efficiency and get better results."[19] And steps have indeed been taken in an effort to reform DOE's contracting procedures. Since the National Performace Review, the department has been working to negotiate contracts that it hopes will provide greater incentives for efficiency than do M&O contracts, and new contracts are indeed in place at two of EM's largest sites—Rocky Flats in Colorado and the Idaho National Engineering Laboratory, as well as at several smaller sites. But as this monograph goes to press, more than 70 percent of EM dollars are still being spent on work governed by M&O contracts.[20]

17. Ibid.
18. Ibid., pp. 6–7.
19. O'Leary, "The Department of Energy: Why Abolishment Makes No Sense," p. 8.
20. Some improvements in efficiency may come of DOE's initiative to privatize certain aspects of the cleanup. Under this arrangement, contractors obtain private financing for undertaking cleanup tasks and receive payment only after a job is completed. Whether this effort will prove successful, however, is far from clear. Work at DOE's Idaho National Engineering Laboratory has now been privatized, for example, but the contractor has not completed work on time and "DOE's officials acknowledged that while the privatization concept generally calls for the contractor to take responsibility for all project foul-ups, the department could still get stuck paying these penalties due to vague accountability provisions in the . . . contract" (George Lobsenz, "Idaho Officials Say Cleanup Privatization No Panacea," *Energy Daily*, March 19, 1996, p. 1).

Furthermore, reports of waste and mismanagement continue. In March 1995, some two years after the National Performance Review, a report requested of two former DOE officials by the Senate Energy and Natural Resources Committee on cleanup efforts at DOE's largest site, in Hanford, Washington, charged that much of its $1.5 billion annual budget is being "squandered. . . . There is almost no aspect of the current program . . . that can withstand close scrutiny. The current process is not working effectively, the site is spending more money than it can justify, and no reliable date exists for completing the cleanup"[21] In the same month, the *Wall Street Journal* reported that, "many workers [at Hanford] . . . complain that there are three people for every job."[22] And a General Accounting Office study of "productivity improvements" at EM (reforms undertaken as part of the initiative that included the National Performance Review) found that DOE's headquarters accepted most projected savings figures from its field offices despite a review of those projections that found that nearly 90 percent of their promised savings were "not adequately justified."[23]

The secretary rightly argues that DOE is constrained by "deadlines and commitments codified in 81 enforceable compliance agreements with 23 states."[24] But the March 1995 report on Hanford points out that DOE has not taken the initiative in challenging this regulatory structure: "DOE has accepted decisions by its environmental regulators even when both the Department and its contractors believe the decisions lack technical validity . . . Congress cannot look to

---

21. Steven M. Blush and Thomas H. Heitman, *Train Wreck along the River of Money: An Evaluation of the Hanford Cleanup,* report for the U.S. Senate Committee on Energy and Natural Resources, March 1995, pp. 3–4.
22. Timothy Aeppel, "Untidy Cleanup: Mess at A-Bomb Plant Shows What Happens If Pork Gets into Play," *Wall Street Journal,* March 28, 1995.
23. U.S. General Accounting Office, *Environmental Management: Impact of Increases in DOE's Workforce,* GAO/RCED-95-207, July 1995, p. 5.
24. O'Leary, "The Department of Energy: Why Abolishment Makes No Sense," p. 7.

DOE to change the existing process." Nor has DOE stood up to wasteful contractors: a recent report by the department's inspector general slammed DOE for allowing itself to be bullied into paying tens of millions of dollars in excess fees to Westinghouse for work at its Savannah River site.[25]

In short, DOE's inability to cope with the cleanup problem has survived both Republican and Democratic administrations and numerous departmental reorganizations. Secretary O'Leary's initiative is the latest effort to put things right by injecting incentives into the contracting system, cutting the number of contractors, reducing their travel bills, and otherwise tweaking DOE's cleanup program. Laudable as these goals may be, it would seem to any observer with a sense of history that these reforms are unlikely to convert "a grand and glorious mess," in which administrative overheads consume huge resources but contractors are nevertheless not effectively supervised, into an efficiently managed cleanup program.

That the intrinsic difficulty of the cleanup is exacerbated by a web of state and federal laws and deadlines, no one can doubt. That the lack of clear political direction in such matters as the acceptable level of site restoration complicates DOE's problem is beyond question. And that the solutions to the problems of successfully operating a massive contractor program are not self-evident is also clear. But that DOE has failed, miserably, under well-meaning secretaries with different backgrounds and political orientations is the most glaring fact. "The cleanup," the report on Hanford concluded, "is already terribly complex and yet DOE has been adding organizational complexity on top of the existing technical complexity."[26] Even allowing for the technical and legal burdens imposed on DOE, it has not efficiently disposed of its

---

25. See U.S. Department of Energy, Office of Inspector General, *Report on Inspection of Westinghouse Savannah River Company Fees for Managing and Operating the Savannah River Site*, August 1995.
26. Blush and Heitman, *Train Wreck along the River of Money*, p. ES-6.

cleanup duties, nor has it taken the lead in reforming the incoherent and contradictory legal framework within which the cleanup must now take place.

In short, it would do no harm to the cleanup program—and would quite possibly improve its efficiency and effectiveness—to transfer it out of DOE. Indeed, in a recent General Accounting Office survey of energy policy experts—including four former secretaries of energy and President Carter—nearly two in three (including some in favor of retaining DOE and some in favor of abolishing the department) favored this action.[27] A smaller agency charged solely with carrying out DOE's defense-related responsibilities could focus on these duties without also concerning itself with "providing the scientific foundation, technology, policy, and institutional leadership necessary to achieve efficiency in energy use, diversity in energy sources . . . [and] a more productive and competitive economy"—the rest of DOE's sweeping mission. Whether this agency should report to the Department of Defense, in the same way that the Federal Energy Regulatory Commission is now an independent agency within DOE, is a question to be decided by those with greater expertise in these organizational details.

National Security. DOE's national security programs include the Office of Defense Programs, the Office of Nonproliferation and National Security, the Office of Fissile Materials Disposition, and the Office of Nuclear Energy, Science, and Techology; the last group devotes a portion of its budget to civilian activities. In all, national security activities consume about $4.9 billion, nearly a third of DOE's 1996 budget. Most important, accounting for some $3.4 billion, is the Office of Defense Programs. This office, which controls the second largest portion of DOE's budget (after the Office of Environmental Management),

---

27. U.S. General Accounting Office, *Department of Energy: A Framework for Restructuring DOE and Its Missions,* GAO/RCED-95-197, August 1995, pp. 25–26.

manages the nation's stockpile of nuclear weapons and directs the weapons-related research conducted at three of DOE's national laboratories. The much smaller Office of Nonproliferation and National Security, with a budget of a bit over a half-billion dollars, is charged with sharing DOE's technical knowledge with federal intelligence agencies and helping prevent nuclear proliferation, including verification of treaty compliance and monitoring weapons and weapons-usable materials in the former Soviet Union. The Office of Fissile Materials Disposition, with a $70 million budget, is responsible for storing and managing enriched, weapons-usable plutonium and uranium originally intended for nuclear weapons or taken from dismantled nuclear weapons. Finally, DOE's Office of Nuclear Energy, Science, and Technology spends about $700 million annually on defense-related activities, with the bulk devoted to work in naval reactors.

Since none of these functions can be eliminated, the practical question becomes whether DOE or some other agency is the proper repository for them. All the arguments recited in favor of a separate agency for waste management apply here. In addition, if it is decided that DOE's civilian programs should be transferred, eliminated, or privatized (as we recommend), transfer of its national security functions would permit closing down the department altogether, with possible additional savings in administrative costs.

Some have proposed transferring these functions to the Department of Defense. To attempt to decide that difficult question would take us beyond the scope of this report. But we do note that one argument against such a move is that it runs counter to a long-standing policy of keeping the development and maintenance of nuclear weapons firmly under civilian control.[28] This policy is based in part on the fear that the military, eager to maxi-

---

28. See Charles B. Curtis, under secretary of energy, U.S. Department of Energy, Statement before the Committee on National Security, Subcommittee on Military Procurement, March 25, 1995 (mimeo), pp. 2–3.

mize the bang from each buck, will be inclined to devote a smaller portion of the available resources to safety considerations than would a civilian-controlled organization.

As stated in the recently released report of the Galvin Task Force on the national laboratories, this argument goes as follows:

> The separation, within the U.S. government, of nuclear weapons development and operations is a long tradition and has recently been challenged in the interest of efficiency. . . . The Task Force, however . . . believes that there is much value at this time in maintaining an independent and technically expert organization to focus on nuclear stockpile issues and to continue to ensure that decisions regarding the safety, control, and stewardship of nuclear weapons are raised to the high policy level that they deserve.[29]

Those favoring continued civilian control also contend that the Defense Department is not the place to look for innovative research. Thus, Edward Teller of Livermore National Laboratory recently testified:

> A military research effort outside the Pentagon may be particularly useful at this time. Big organizations such as the Defense Department are conservative in their nature, and even more so when budgets are declining. Therefore, radically new initiatives of great potential importance are apt to arise outside of such big organizations. For such reasons, I suggest that military developments in the Department of Energy continue, moreover across a broad front.[30]

29. Task Force on Alternative Futures for the Department of Energy Laboratories, *Alternative Futures for the Department of Energy Laboratories,* February 1995 (Hereinafter, Galvin Report), pp. 16–17.
30. Edward Teller, Statement before the House Subcommittee on Energy and Water Development of the Committee on Appropriations, U.S. House of Representatives, January 31, 1995, in *Energy and Water Development Appropriations for 1996,* p. 861.

We are in no position to determine the validity of the technical aspects of these arguments. But several points seem to have been overlooked by those who worry about maintaining civilian control of the weapons program. First, the Defense Department *is* under the control of a civilian secretary of defense who reports directly to the president. Second, it is possible to maintain independent civilian control of the programs now operated by DOE even if they are lodged within the Defense Department. Furthermore, Dr. Teller's fear that large organizations, particularly those faced with declining budgets, are too "conservative," seems to miss an important point: DOE is just such an organization—large, and with a declining budget. Furthermore, if by *conservative* Dr. Teller means that agencies under budgetary pressure tend to choose their research targets more carefully, to act as if money matters, and to say no to projects that do not meet the market-related tests we suggest below, it may well be that a bit of "conservatism" would separate some research chaff from the wheat.

In short, continued civilian control of the weapons program does not mandate the continued existence of DOE. And that department's perpetual management problems—of which the current secretary's peripatetic proclivities are only the most recent and, in the end, a relatively trivial example—and the overhead costs associated with its continued existence point to a transfer of its weapons responsibilities to some other agency, especially if such a move facilitates the department's elimination.

Civilian Programs

The civilian programs managed by DOE consumed some $6.2 billion in 1996. Although the department's organizational maze makes it difficult to classify these programs functionally, a workable if slightly imprecise categorization is as follows: civilian radioactive waste management; scientific research; technology transfer; energy supply

R&D (fossil, nuclear, renewables, and efficiency); asset management; data gathering and publication; education; and regulation.

Civilian Radioactive Waste Management. The Office of Civilian Radioactive Waste Management (OCRWM) was established by the Nuclear Waste Policy Act of 1982 to manage the disposal of spent nuclear fuel from commercial reactors, as well as some high-level radioactive waste from nuclear weapons production.

OCRWM was budgeted $400 million in 1996; roughly the same amount is requested for 1997. The program is funded almost entirely from two sources—the Nuclear Waste Fund and the Defense Nuclear Waste Appropriation. The former was established by the 1982 law: power companies collect the mandated sums from their ratepayers, and then pay that money into the fund to have the waste from their nuclear plants stored in the OCRWM repository. The Defense Nuclear Waste Appropriation, which began in 1993, is a transfer of funds from DOE's Office of Defense Programs to cover the cost of storing some weapons-related waste that finds its way into the civilian repository. Both utility ratepayers and the Office of Defense Programs pay into the fund in proportion to the costs DOE estimates each imposes on the system.

OCRWM is in the process of "characterizing" a site for a deep underground repository to hold nuclear waste for tens of thousands of years. That site, Yucca Mountain in Nevada, was selected by Congress. Thus far, DOE has spent some $4.5 billion "characterizing" the Yucca Mountain site. But progress in constructing the repository has been somewhere between zero and nil.

OCRWM originally announced plans to open the facility in 1998 and signed contracts with utilities based on that schedule.[31] But, as is the case with other DOE pro-

---

31. U.S. Department of Energy, *Civilian Radioactive Waste Management Program Plan: Program Overview,* December 19, 1994, pp. 4–5.

grams, the civilian nuclear waste management program has been afflicted by cost overruns and delays. An "intensive review" revealed what OCRWM's director calls "significant disparities" among the program's goals, resources, and achievements—and, typically elicited promises to do better.[32] DOE's public position is that the repository will open in 2010, but knowledgeable industry observers say that 2016 is a more likely date. So the electric utilities are pressing Congress for legislation that would in fact as well as in appearance authorize the construction of an interim "monitored retrievable storage" facility by 1998, at which time the companies expect the waste from their nuclear power plants to exceed their temporary storage capacity.

And therein lies a possible solution. Private utilities are under the greatest pressure to develop permanent storage facilities for their nuclear waste. Should they run out of storage space, they face the prospect of a costly closure of their nuclear plants, which, once closed, might be removed from their rate bases on the grounds that they are no longer "used and useful," to use regulators' parlance.

In addition to their incentive to solve the problem, the utilities have long (if imperfect) experience with coordinated efforts in research, through the Electric Power Research Institute, and in facilities planning and management (transmission systems, power pools). Such experience would enable the utilities themselves to organize, build, and operate (subject, of course, to attaining specified safety standards) a waste repository if freed to do so by the government.

And they would have every incentive to do so at the minimum cost consistent with such safety regulations as the government might establish. For the power generation business is now sufficiently competitive to have eliminated any relaxed attitude utilities might once have had to the level of their costs. Indeed, the utilities' regulators, represented by the National Association of Regulatory Utility Commissioners, no natural ally of private utilities,

---

32. Ibid., p. ix.

are becoming so concerned with OCRWM's waste of rate-payers' funds that they are coming to favor allowing the electric companies to take over the chore of establishing a waste repository. And they are not alone: the General Accounting Office, the Office of Technology Assessment, several independent commissions and a coalition including both electric utility executives and regulators have endorsed privatizing civilian radioactive waste disposal.[33]

Surely, the presence of an incentive to solve the storage problem, experience with cooperative facilities construction and management, and market pressures to minimize costs, all combine to create an environment in which a private sector effort has every chance of success. If DOE is eliminated, this option is worthy of serious exploration before turning the OCRWM program over to some other government agency or corporation.

Scientific Research. DOE's research is carried out, by and large, at universities and at the department's national laboratories, which are owned by the government but operated by private contractors. This research includes seeking what DOE calls "a deeper understanding of the nature of matter and energy" through its "High Energy and Nuclear Physics Programs"; work to provide "a fundamental scientific foundation for the Nation's future energy options"; the development of "the knowledge base" necessary to conduct research into environmental and health matters and scientific problems in medicine and biology; and work on fusion energy.[34]

Any appraisal of the proper scope of tax-funded research must begin with a consideration of appropriability. As a joint committee of the National Academy of Sciences, the National Academy of Engineering, and the Institute of Medicine put it in a 1992 report on this subject:

33. Pamela Newman, "Coalition Pushes Controversial Waste Privatization Proposal," *Energy Daily,* March 23, 1995.

34. U.S. Department of Energy, *Programs of the Office of Energy Research,* September 1992, pp. 3, 16, 24, 33.

Private companies have little financial incentive to invest in R&D that will be available outside the company and therefore involves significant problems in appropriability for the firm. It is when scientific inquiry involves the promise of useful new knowledge that is generic in nature, with wide applications across economic activities, and there are insufficient private returns to investment in R&D, that governments must act.[35]

Most scholars support this view. Julian M. Alston and Philip G. Pardey, for example, in *Making Science Pay: The Economics of Agricultural R&D Policy*, examine federal spending on USDA agricultural research programs and draw conclusions that are pertinent here. They favor continued federal spending on R&D:

The main reason is appropriability. Often those who invest in R&D cannot capture all the benefits—others can "free ride" on an investment in research, using the results and sharing in the benefits without sharing in the costs. When private returns are less than returns to the society as a whole, the private sector will underinvest in research from the nation's point of view.[36]

This distinction between research, the benefits of which can be appropriated by private parties, and research that results in innovations that cannot be appropriated seems to us a more useful one than the more conventional distinction between basic and applied research. As a recent report on DOE's R&D efforts points out, "The distinction between basic and applied research breaks down in reality. . . . What the government calls 'applied R&D' . . . is

35. Committee on Science, Engineering, and Public Policy, *The Government Role in Civilian Technology: Building a New Alliance* (Washington, D.C.: National Academy Press, 1992), p. 19.
36. Julian M. Alston and Philip G. Pardey, *Making Science Pay: The Economics of Agricultural R&D Policy* (Washington, D.C.: AEI Press, 1996), p. 231.

often called 'basic research' by private companies."[37]

Attempts to distinguish "basic research," presumably a legitimate claimant on taxpayer funds, from "applied research," or even "development," even when successful, are of little use for policy purposes. Instead, consider how a distinction between sufficiently appropriable research and research that creates problems of appropriability might help in defining the limits of government involvement, using DOE's current research establishment as a test case.

Some of DOE's current research projects are likely to lead to commercially appropriable results. Private parties are in a good position to identify those projects. If DOE were required to offer rights to its various research projects, at auction, appropriable research would pass to the private sector. That would relieve the government of responsibility for further funding of those projects. Rules appropriate to such an auction might be complicated, but no more so than those established by the government for spectrum auctions.

Simultaneously, the possibility of revising the patent laws to increase the range of appropriable research should be considered. The goal would be to increase appropriability sufficiently to stimulate private sector research, without going so far as to retard unduly the economic diffusion of new discoveries.

Finally, the costs and likely benefits of that residuum of projects in which the private sector shows no interest, either because their costs genuinely exceed conceivable benefits, because intellectual property rights cannot be protected, or because "public benefits, such as national security . . . are simply not fully reflected in market prices,"[38] should be com-

---

37. Secretary of Energy Advisory Board, Task Force on Strategic Energy Research and Development, *Energy R&D: Shaping Our Nation's Future in a Competitive World,* June 1995, p. 10.

38. U.S. Department of Energy, Office of Policy, *Success Stories: The Energy Mission in the Marketplace* (Hereinafter, *Success Stories),* Annex 3 to Task Force on Strategic Energy Research and Development, *Energy R&D,* p. 171.

pared with those of all government-funded projects, not merely with those now conducted under the aegis of DOE. It may well be that there are more urgent demands on the public purse than DOE's research projects, a distinct possibility given the department's recent infatuation with "technology partnerships" such as the Partnership for a New Generation of Vehicles, a subsidy to profitable auto makers.

DOE's argument in support of continuing its research activities is not limited to a citation of problems of appropriability. It goes further. The department asserts that the existence of substantial market failure causes underinvestment by the private sector in "applied energy R&D programs," requiring DOE to "fill an important gap in the United States' R&D continuum":

> In today's highly competitive global market, technical secrets are short-lived and too easily stolen, scientists are hired away, and inventions are slightly modified in order to circumvent intellectual property rights. More fundamentally, the R&D itself is often too challenging, requiring large interdisciplinary teams of scientists, working year after year on expensive and unique laboratory equipment. Finally, the structure of certain industries is just too fragmented, or the firms too small, to mount the sustained R&D campaign necessary for success.[39]

Criticisms of its research efforts recently prompted DOE to reappraise its programs.[40] Unfortunately, in that assessment, the department failed to develop a framework of analysis that might delineate the government's role in scientific research not directly related to its core missions from that of the private sector. According to the report, DOE laboratories "are called upon to provide broad-based research

---

39. Ibid.
40. U.S. Department of Energy, Laboratory Operations Board, *Draft Strategic Laboratory Missions Plan,* March 1996, vols. 1 and 2.

programs" and "are well positioned to formulate and bring to fruition complex scientific programs that are in the national interest."[41] No retreat from earlier claims to a role so broadly defined as to permit DOE to conduct just about any research and development programs that strike its fancy.

These are certainly arguments too far. If DOE really believes that today's "highly competitive global market" stifles the incentive to conduct research, it is seriously out of touch with reality. Most corporations are engaged in frantic efforts to develop "knowledge bases" (to use a DOE term) from which to launch profitable new products, ranging from life-prolonging pharmaceuticals to knowledge-diffusing communications technologies. Venture capitalists vie to provide funds to genetic research firms that will spend many years and many millions before turning a profit, if they ever do, giving the lie to arguments that private sector firms look only to the short term. And as for small firms being unable to fund R&D, DOE might profit from a conversation with Bill Gates.

This is not to say that market failure is never a problem. Research with no presently discernible application, often expensive, complex, and long term in character, might indeed be suboptimally funded by the private sector. But that does not automatically justify federal intervention, especially by an agency whose system of national laboratories has been criticized in several recent reports for lack of direction, for inept management, and for excessive overhead costs.[42] For against the possibility of market failure must be set the possibility of governmental failure, witness the department's efforts at technology transfer.

Technology Transfer. DOE sees its mission not only as providing basic research and "pre-commercial, applied R&D,"

41. Ibid., vol. 1, p. 42.
42. See the Galvin Report; Task Force on Strategic Energy Research and Development, *Energy R&D;* and U.S. General Accounting Office, *Department of Energy: National Laboratories Need Clearer Missions and Better Management,* GAO/RCED-95-10, January 1995.

where the market fails to do so, but also as facilitating the transfer of knowledge gained from these endeavors to commercial uses. To this end, DOE's Office of Technology Partnerships and Economic Competitiveness took on the "goal of bolstering U.S. economic competitiveness in the global marketplace,"[43] thereby improving job prospects and living standards. That office was subsumed in 1995 into the Office of Research and Development Management, which in turn was abolished in 1996. But the expenditures continue, although at a lower level: DOE now sets aside $165 million annually for "technology transfer"—the collaboration of government scientists and private firms on applied research projects that are beneficial to the private sector.[44] Ostensibly, DOE has carefully defined its role:

> The proper role for the U.S. Department of Energy's applied R&D programs is *not* to subsidize or displace private sector responsibilities for R&D, but to complement them selectively in ways that will help achieve long term public policy objectives. [emphasis in original][45]

In practice, however, DOE has considerable difficulty in avoiding subsidization and displacement of private sector efforts. Consider one program for technology transfer—Cooperative Research and Development Agreements (CRADAs), used by DOE, among other government agencies. CRADAs allow private firms to pool resources with federal laboratories in pursuit of mutual research goals. But it is difficult to know whether companies are using CRADAs to support research that they would in any event fund or whether they are undertaking research that would not be conducted without government support. According to Richard Quisenberry, a former DuPont executive who

---

43. U.S. Department of Energy, *U.S. Department of Energy: What Is It? What Does It Do?* p. 7.
44. U.S. Department of Energy, *Laboratory Operations Board, Draft Strategic Laboratory Missions Plan,* vol. 2, pp. NS-27 and ST-48.
45. U.S. Department of Energy, *Success Stories,* p. 171.

manages a group of textile firms working with government labs, "My quarrel with a lot of CRADAs is that they are . . . marginal things that industry could do, but if they can get the government to go halvers with them, they'll go that way instead."[46]

Alexander MacLachlan, then deputy under secretary for technology partnerships, took a contrary view. He defends the value of these partnerships by pointing out "the surge in repeat business" of companies conducting applied research using federal grants: "People would not keep coming back to us if they didn't see value."[47] True: and it is no surprise that many businesses "see value" in having DOE cover a portion of the research costs that they, in the absence of such subsidy, would have to bear in full.

In reaction to criticism, DOE has touted its "success stories"—such technologies as high-efficiency lights, windows, and other appliances that have benefited the public.[48] But those tales beg the question of whether DOE is displacing private sector R&D. A recent series of articles in the *Philadelphia Inquirer* suggests just such displacement on a large scale. DOE researchers helped develop suntan lotion for a New York–based firm, enhance a dry-cleaning process at a Kansas City business, maintain an assembly line for the makers of Dove ice-cream bars, and improve the fireworks at Disneyworld.[49] In short, it certainly seems arguable that DOE's role is often "to subsidize or displace private sector responsibilities for R&D," exactly the consequence it claims to avoid. Little wonder that the Galvin Task Force

---

46. Gilbert Gaul and Susan Stranahan, "The Price of Keeping Labs Busy," *Philadelphia Inquirer,* June 5, 1995.

47. Alexander MacLachlan, deputy under secretary for technology partnerships, U.S. Department of Energy, Statement before the Subcommittee on Energy and Water Development of the Committee on Appropriations, U.S. House of Representatives, March 9, 1995, in *Energy and Water Development Appropriations for 1996,* p. 512.

48. See U.S. Department of Energy, *Success Stories.*

49. Gaul and Stranahan, "The Price of Keeping Labs Busy," and "How Billions in Taxes Failed to Create New Jobs," *Philadelphia Inquirer,* June 4 and 5, 1995.

characterized these and related activities as "unfocused and lack[ing] a firm policy foundation" and "unlikely to produce results that will benefit either the agency's industrial partners or the public in the long run."[50]

Energy Supply R&D. When President Carter and Congress established DOE in 1977, it was fashionable to believe that existing energy resources were limited, that soaring demand was pressing on a dwindling supply of oil and natural gas, and that environmental problems placed unavoidable limits on growth. Wrong then, this diagnosis is clearly wrong now, when both oil and gas are and promise to remain available in ample quantities.

Yet DOE persists in devoting taxpayer funds to expanding energy supply—and it does so in areas that should clearly be left to private sector development. DOE's nuclear energy research has been described by the deputy director of its Office of Nuclear Energy, Science, and Technology as covering a range of subjects, some of them properly categorized as defense and security related. "Most prominently," though, he says, "we are working to maintain the nuclear option for the country . . . in a cost-shared program to design a new safer and economical generation of nuclear energy plants."[51] That this relieves GE and Westinghouse of research burdens no one can doubt. That it is the business of DOE thus to subsidize the private sector is less certain. And that there is a need for such a program is questionable: "the wisdom of pursuing new technologies [for nuclear energy] is questionable as long as electric utilities, the intended recipients, have no interest in new nuclear plants."[52]

---

50. Galvin Report, p. 45.

51. Ray Hunter, acting deputy director, Office of Nuclear Energy, U.S. Department of Energy, Statement before the Subcommittee on Energy and Water Development of the Committee on Appropriations, U.S. House of Representatives, March 14, 1995, in *Energy and Water Development Appropriations for 1996*, p. 825.

52. Congressional Budget Office, *Reducing the Deficit: Spending and Revenue Options*. Report to the Senate and House Committees on the Budget, February 1995, p. 110.

So, too, with DOE's fossil energy research. Its Office of Fossil Energy hunts for "innovations in [oil] exploration and production technologies," has spent $2.5 billion developing techniques for making coal "more environmentally acceptable," and has developed "improved extraction techniques" for natural gas.[53] Why the oil, coal, and natural gas industries have insufficient means or incentives to engage in such research is as difficult to ascertain as is the reason that "DOE continues to develop technologies in which the market clearly has no interest."[54]

The department's inability to self-limit its research role is demonstrated by its request for a 37 percent increase in funds for "solar and renewable" energy programs (FY 1997 request, over FY 1996 appropriation), areas the Congressional Budget Office characterizes in many cases as having "a clear enough market to warrant private investment."[55] In the past, DOE's litany of reasons for such expenditures has included "strengthening the Nation's energy security, promoting sustainable energy approaches . . . increasing U.S. industrial competitiveness," and attaining "the goal of tripling the non-hydropower renewable energy capacity by the year 2000."[56] Central planning redux: DOE gears its R&D to the roles it believes each energy source should play in the nation's overall supply picture.

Which brings us to the department's Office of Energy Efficiency and Renewable Energy. If, as DOE contends, renewable energy systems are "better and ready for business,"[57] DOE should suspend its support and leave it to the private sector to introduce these systems. If, however, these technologies cannot compete in a market in which fossil fuels are abundant and cheap, and in which information is

---

53. U.S. Department of Energy, *The Office of Fossil Energy*, January 1994, p.1; and *Clean Coal Technology: The Investment Pays Off* (n.d.), p. 1.
54. Congressional Budget Office, *Reducing the Deficit*, p. 110.
55. Ibid., p. 111.
56. Department of Energy, *FY 1997 Congressional Budget Request*, p. 54.
57. U.S. Department of Energy, *Energy for Today and Tomorrow: Investments for a Strong America, Fiscal Year 1996 Budget in Brief*, p. 3.

now widely available to consumers, they should be treated as anachronisms, relics of the days when we feared oil prices of $100 per barrel and shortages of natural gas. DOE claims that "American consumers and businesses could be saving $38 billion annually on their energy bills,"[58] but for some reason are not and need the department's Office of Building Technologies to show the way. Perhaps consumers were inattentive to such savings when the first oil crisis struck over twenty years ago, but no such information gap, or market failure, exists now. Facilities managers are quite capable of deciding the economically optimal use of energy, and consumers who care to find out know which autos use how much fuel, which refrigerators cost more or less to operate, and what trade-off between first cost and operating cost most closely reflects their private discount rates.

Asset Management. There is bipartisan consensus that DOE should divest itself of most of the energy-generating assets it now holds, which include oil fields, power marketing administrations, and petroleum reserves.

DOE owns six oil fields—three naval petroleum reserves and three naval oil shale reserves—located in California, Colorado, Utah, and Wyoming. The largest of the fields, Elk Hills Naval Petroleum Reserve in California, produces 65,000 barrels of oil per day, making it one of the ten largest U.S. oil fields outside of Alaska.[59] The idea for government ownership of oil fields came from President Theodore Roosevelt, who foresaw the need for a reserve of oil to supply the U.S. Navy, which was then switching from coal- to oil-powered vessels. The first fields were reserved to the government under President William Howard Taft.[60] The reserves have long since ceased to serve any naval pur-

---

58. Ibid., p. 10.
59. U.S. Department of Energy, *Naval Petroleum and Oil Shale Reserves: Annual Report of Operations, Fiscal Year 1993*, 1994, p. 9.
60. National Academy of Public Administration, *Restructuring the Naval Petroleum and Oil Shale Reserves: A Report of the Department of Energy*, April 1994, p. 5.

pose; indeed, production from these fields was negligible between the end of World War II and the energy crises of the 1970s. When the embargoes hit, output was increased, in the case of Elk Hills to its current level of production. Of course, had Elk Hills and the other naval reserves been in private hands, that oil would have been equally available to offset lost imports. It was not government ownership, but the existence of the reserves, that made the oil available.

The end of the crises did not result in reduced production from the naval reserves: the government came to count on the revenues from the oil sales and has maintained output at crisis levels.

But oil production, clearly, is normally "a highly competitive part of the private sector,"[61] as Presidents Reagan, Bush, and Clinton have recognized by calling for the sale of these reserves. That call, supported by Secretary O'Leary, has now been heeded. Under recently enacted legislation, DOE is proceeding with divestiture of Elk Hills, which, under a best-case scenario, will be in the private sector by 1998. The fate of the other five fields, which collectively produce a fraction of the output of Elk Hills, is less clear.

The administration's proposal to privatize or partially privatize the five power marketing administrations held by DOE, which sell power generated by dams and other federal facilities, has not met with similar success. The PMAs include the massive Bonneville Power Administration, which markets power from dams along the Columbia River to the Pacific Northwest; the Southeastern Power Administration; the Southwestern Power Administration; the Western Area Power Administration; and the Alaskan Power Administration. Together, these administrations supply 6 percent of the nation's power, until recently at below-market rates, from about 130 government-held facilities in thirty-four states.[62] Although the PMAs are

61. Ibid., p. 11.
62. "Energy Assets Privatization: Transfer PMAs to the Private Sector," Alliance for Power Privatization news release, March 28, 1995.

charged with paying back all loans to the federal government, this is done over such a long term and at such low interest rates as to amount to a de facto subsidy.

Many Republicans and Democrats agree on the wisdom of selling the PMAs, although the recent defeat of bipartisan efforts to do just that (sale of the tiny Alaska Power Administration is the exception) attests to the political clout of those who have benefited from subsidized power. The only difference of opinion on this issue between the Clinton administration and a task force of congressional Republicans that has called for DOE's elimination, for example, is over whether Bonneville should be converted into a government-held corporation or privatized outright.[63] Still, there is opposition to the sale in Congress, even among some Republicans. One first-term House Republican advocates eliminating the Energy Department, as well as the Departments of Commerce, Education, and Housing and Urban Development, and favors dramatically scaling back welfare and federal support for the arts. But she opposes privatization of Bonneville, claiming it would "destroy the economy" of the Northwest, where Bonneville's subsidized power has been available at half the national average price to aluminum factories operating in her Washington district.[64]

We agree with a colleague of hers who points out that, for the nation as a whole, "many more people will win if we privatize these agencies. . . . Maybe selling Bonneville would raise rates in the Northwest, but it might

---

63. Both the administration and the Energy Task Force (the group of nine House Republicans formed to eliminate DOE) have proposed privatizing the other four PMAs. See "DOE Alignment Delivers $1.7 Billion to Taxpayers," DOE news release, May 3, 1995; cover page, Office of the Vice President, *From Red Tape to Results,* pp. 41–44; and "Department of Energy Abolishment Act: Legislative Summary," Energy Task Force news release, June 8, 1995, Title III.
64. Timothy Egan, "A G.O.P. Attack Hits Bit Too Close to Home," *New York Times,* March 3, 1995. Indeed, it is quite possible that the real policy issue relates to how to introduce competition into the Bonneville area, so that customers can choose between its power and that of new, low-cost producers.

reduce rates in California."[65] In an era in which competition among electric utilities for customers is feasible, subsidizing some of those competitors—the power marketing administrations—has an increasingly distorting effect on the efficiency with which resources are allocated. It is unclear why regions without federal power should be asked to subsidize low electric rates in areas served by PMAs, particularly when this subsidy confers an advantage in luring business from other parts of the country. And that the initiative to sell the PMAs has largely fizzled is particularly striking in light of the worldwide privatization of nearly $40 billion worth of power assets in the past eight years. This figure includes nations as diverse as Brazil, Hungary, the United Kingdom, and Malaysia—but not the United States.[66]

Finally, DOE holds the Strategic Petroleum Reserve, which contains nearly 600 billion barrels of crude oil held for use in the event of an oil supply crisis. The reserve, located along the Gulf Coast in Louisiana and Texas, was built in response to the oil embargo of 1973 and can hold up to one trillion barrels of oil. This is not the place to review its management and mismanagement. But a December 1994 report from the Congressional Budget Office questions whether changes in oil markets, including greater flexibility in oil use and prices, do not make "the benefits from releasing SPR oil in an oil crisis . . . smaller today than in the past."[67] One thing is clear: no one is prepared to defend the efficiency with which the SPR has been operated. Little would be lost, and something might be gained, by transferring it to another agency.

65. Ibid.
66. Douglas A. Houston, *Federal Power: The Case for Privatizing Electricity,* Reason Foundation Policy Study No. 201, March 1996, p. 11.
67. Congressional Budget Office, *Rethinking Emergency Energy Policy,* December 1994, p. ix.

Data-gathering, Publication, Education, and Regulation.
The Energy Information Administration collects and publishes data on energy resources, production, demand, consumption, and distribution. Whether this function should be transferred to another agency, or left to the plethora of private data gatherers now cramming the information superhighway with their wares, should be determined after soliciting advice from producers and consumers of the data being gathered. The functions of the recently eliminated Office of Science Education and Technical Information—to coordinate DOE's university science education programs and publish information about the department's R&D activities—continue within the Office of Energy Research. Were DOE dismantled, both functions might be reviewed and, if essential, transferred to the National Science Foundation.

The Federal Energy Regulatory Commission, already an independent agency within DOE, could easily exist outside the agency. The need for FERC as it is currently constituted should be reexamined at the time of its transfer from DOE. Despite the end of staff-intensive natural gas price regulation, FERC has maintained the same staffing levels that existed when it was charged with determining just and reasonable natural gas prices. It now faces another revolution: emerging competition in the electric utility industry, a development that promises to reduce the need for regulatory (as opposed to antitrust) oversight. The occasion of FERC's transfer from DOE should be used for a thorough reappraisal of that agency's staffing needs.

4

Conclusions

The Department of Energy should be abolished, some of its functions eliminated, some privatized, and some transferred to other agencies. Repeated efforts at reform, by successive administrations and secretaries, have failed to eliminate inefficient contracting procedures, to focus DOE's sprawling research effort, or to persuade its bureaucracy to stop meddling in energy markets.

These conclusions arise from an analysis of the department's activities, rather than from any antigovernment ideology or mere desire to reduce government spending: they would not be different were the federal budget now in surplus.

One legitimate concern remains to be considered: the costs of transferring functions from DOE to other departments. If these transfers are to involve more than changing the signs on the doors of the Forrestal Building and printing new letterheads and business cards for the existing DOE bureaucracy, the inheritor agencies will require new people, new management technologies, and a learning period. That the transition costs will be worth bearing is suggested by the appalling inability of a succession of well-meaning and honorable DOE secretaries to bring coherence to the department's programs. That is a fair inference from numerous assessments of DOE's performance in its various spheres of activity. Vice President

Al Gore's National Performance Review found DOE's cleanup efforts to be inefficient, and DOE has not produced evidence of improved efficiency since that report's publication. As for the department's R&D program, even as enthusiastic a set of supporters as the secretary's Task Force on Strategic Energy Research and Development finds that "DOE's bureaucracy and many of its policies and procedures impose large costs upon the performance of energy R&D under federal sponsorship," citing "overlapping management contracts, duplicative laboratory programs, marginal and overlapping research projects and facilities, and programs not directly related to strategic DOE energy R&D missions."[1] And DOE's energy supply program is incoherent, spending millions on technologies for which there are no markets and more millions on efforts best left to the private sector.

Although we respect Secretary O'Leary's attempts to respond to these criticisms, history suggests—indeed, more than suggests—that radical improvement is impossible within the culture of DOE. The department simply cannot do well what must be done and persists in doing things best left to the private sector. Secretary O'Leary is merely the latest in a long line that would change all this. But others, equally able, have tried; all have failed, broken on the reef of the department's entrenched procedures and bureaucracy.

In short, DOE cannot be reinvented; it must be abolished.

---

1. Task Force on Strategic Energy Research and Development, *Energy R&D*, pp. 37 and 39.

About the Author

IRWIN M. STELZER received his Ph.D. degree from Cornell University and his bachelor's and master's degrees from New York University. He has been director of the Energy and Environmental Policy Centers at Harvard University, an associate member of Nuffield College, Oxford, and a member of the Advisory Panel of the President's National Commission for the Review of Antitrust Laws and Procedures. In addition to his position at the American Enterprise Institute as director of regulatory policy studies, Dr. Stelzer is an honorary fellow of the Centre for Socio-Legal Studies, Oxford, and political and economic columnist for the *Sunday Times* (London) and the *New York Post*. He is the coauthor of *The Antitrust Laws: A Primer* (AEI Press, 1996), now in its second edition.

Dr. Stelzer was assisted by Robert Patton, who received his bachelor's degree in economics and history from the University of Michigan and is currently a research assistant at the American Enterprise Institute.